I. Introduction

An *all-units discount* is a price reduction offered on all units purchased if the customer's total purchases equal or exceed a given quantity threshold. These tariffs are quite common in vertical contracts and have received significant attention from antitrust authorities in recent years. In some cases the discounts are offered at the time of purchase in the form of off-invoice allowances; in other cases they are offered as periodic rebates as quantity thresholds are met. In the latter form, all-units discounts are sometimes called *retroactive rebates*.[2] They have also been defined as one type of *loyalty discount* in the antitrust policy literature.[3]

Since the discount applies to all units rather than only additional units, the tariff exhibits a discontinuous, downward jump—a negative marginal price—at the threshold that triggers the discount. Assuming free disposal, the discontinuity makes it irrational for a customer to purchase a quantity within a specific range below the threshold. For example, if a seller offers a customer a discount of d percent off the list price for total purchases that equal or exceed q units, it does not not make sense for the customer to purchase any quantity from that seller between $(1 - d)q$ and q units. For any purchase in this range, purchasing more would cost less.

The negative marginal price property of all-units discounts has raised concerns among antitrust authorities that these tariffs might harm competition. Consider a downstream firm that currently purchases all of its supplies from an incumbent supplier. If the firm's decision to purchase some amount from a rival supplier would cause its purchases from the incumbent to fall below a discount threshold, the rival may need to compensate the buyer for discounts lost on *inframarginal* units purchased from the incumbent. Based on this logic, the European Union treats all-units discounts by dominant firms as a potential abuse of dominance aimed at excluding competitors.[4]

---

[2]For a discussion of different rebate forms, see European Commission (2009).

[3]See, e.g., Greenlee and Reitman (2005).

[4]All-units discounts are considered a potential abuse of dominance under Article 102 (formerly Article 82) of the Treaty on the Functioning of the European Union. In a review of Article 102, the European Commission states: "In general terms, retroactive rebates may foreclose the market significantly, as they may make it less attractive for customers to switch small amounts of demand to an alternative supplier, if this would lead to loss of the retroactive rebates. ... The higher the rebate as a percentage of the total price and the higher the threshold, the greater the inducement below the threshold, and, therefore, the stronger the likely foreclosure of actual or potential competitors." (European Commission, 2009, paragraph 40).

While all-units discounts are viewed suspiciously by antitrust authorities, the economic rationale for their use is not well-understood. The practice is not mentioned in the two chapters on price discrimination in the Handbook of Industrial Organization.[5] The early agency literature identifies abstract examples in which the optimal payment from a principal to an agent may be a discontinuous function of the principal's revenue,[6] but there has been little systematic work connecting these results to actual tariffs that arise between upstream and downstream firms.[7]

In this paper I offer an explanation for all-units discounts that does not involve exclusionary motives. I consider a vertical relationship in which an upstream and a downstream firm make non-contractible decisions that affect both firms' profits ("double moral hazard"). Prior to these decisions, firms agree to supply terms that may depend on output, but not on investment or pricing decisions. If firms can divide profits with a fixed transfer payment, their objective is to write a contract that induces investment and pricing decisions that maximize joint profits. If the tariff is linear in quantity (a two-part tariff), a conflict arises in attempting to promote both upstream and downstream incentives. A low wholesale price (equal to upstream marginal cost) is required to eliminate double-marginalization and induce efficient downstream investment, but a higher marginal price is required to give the upstream firm an incentive to invest. This conflict prevents two-part tariffs from solving both incentive problems simultaneously.[8]

An intuitive, but incomplete, argument suggests that an all-units discount tariff might be a useful incentive device in this environment. All-units discounts have the merit of providing strong incentives for downstream output expansion while preserving a positive upstream margin that encourages upstream investment. A potential problem with this logic, recognized by Romano (1994)[9], is that the downward jump in an all-units discount tariff introduces an additional moral hazard problem—the upstream firm may be able to shirk on its investment just enough to prevent

---

[5]See Varian (1989) and Stole (2005).

[6]Examples include Lewis (1980) and Singh (1983).

[7]An exception is Kolay et al (2004), discussed below. In canonical models of moral hazard (e.g., Holmstrom, 1979, 1982) and screening (e.g., Maskin and Riley, 1984), payment schedules are typically continuous functions of revenue or quantity.

[8]This conflict was first identified formally by Holmstrom (1982), who showed that sharing rules that do not break the budget (e.g., by paying a penalty to a third party) typically cannot maximize joint profits in team production.

[9]See also Nandeibam (2002).

the downstream firm from reaching the threshold that triggers the discount. When this additional moral hazard is present, the downstream firm will recognize the upstream firm's incentive to shirk and will optimize against the undiscounted price. If upstream investment is a continuous decision variable and the effects of investment on demand are known with certainty (as in Romano's model), all-units discounts are ineffective in the provision of downstream incentives except at the lowest possible level of upstream investment.

In this paper, I consider three variants of the double moral hazard problem in which the positive incentive effects of all-units discounts outweigh the cost of the additional moral hazard they introduce. In the first environment, investment returns are deterministic, as in Romano, but upstream investment is lumpy. Under this assumption, the slight shirking by the upstream firm that undermines all-units discounts when the investment choice is continuous is not feasible. In the second environment, firms are uncertain about the prospects for upstream investment that might arise after contracts are signed ("uncertain prospects"). In the third environment, firms are uncertain about upstream investment returns ("uncertain returns"). Under both uncertain prospects and uncertain returns, the upstream firm's incentive to exploit discontinuities in the tariff is limited because the equilibrium quantity generally differs from the quantity at which the tariff is discontinuous. In all three environments, all-units discounts can arise in equilibrium.

Under lumpy upstream investment with deterministic returns, all-units discounts are optimal tariffs. They support the vertically integrated outcome when upstream costs are sufficiently low, and they distort downstream pricing and investment decisions less than two-part tariffs when investment costs are high. In the optimal all-units discount, the wholesale price exceeds marginal cost at all output levels. The tariff works by giving the retailer the incentive to expand output by enough to receive the discount, while giving the manufacturer sufficient margin to support its investment.

When investment returns are deterministic, declining block tariffs (or the un-dominated portion of a menu of piece-wise linear tariffs) are equivalent to all-units discounts, and thus are also optimal. While both price schedules dominate two-part tariffs, the model is not rich enough to distinguish between continuous and discontinuous tariffs when investment returns are deterministic.

3

However, when investment prospects or returns are uncertain, the tariffs are no longer equivalent. Under these conditions I find two special cases in which all-units discounts achieve the first best outcome, which maximizes joint profits conditional on firms making their pricing and investment decisions before uncertainty is resolved. In these cases—when upstream investment causes an iso-elastic shift in demand, or when the downstream firm's only decision is price—all-units discounts dominate continuous tariffs. The basic logic for all-units discounts in these cases is similar to that in the deterministic case: the discounts simultaneously encourage output expansion by both firms. However, all-units discounts support the efficient outcome in a wider range of cases under uncertain prospects or returns by exploiting the risk experienced by the retailer if it prices too high or invests too little to reach the quantity threshold required to receive the discount.

The antitrust policy question surrounding all-units discounts is whether they can be used to exclude competitors in a way that harms competition. To begin addressing this question in a model in which all-units discounts arise in equilibrium, I introduce the potential for small scale entry in the upstream market, focusing on the deterministic, lumpy upstream investment case. I find that entry by a more efficient competitor is accommodated in equilibrium whether the firms employ all-units discounts or continuous two-block tariffs. Thus, if two-block tariffs are feasible, restricting the use of all-units discounts does not increase the incidence of small scale entry by more efficient competitors in the model considered here. On the other hand, all-units discounts are a poor device for deterring entry by less efficient competitors. Using all-units discounts as an entry deterrent exacerbates the pricing and investment distortions associated with double moral hazard. Two-block tariffs prevent inefficient entry with a smaller distortion than all-units discounts.

A closely-related paper is Romano (1994), which examines the role of resale price maintenance under double moral hazard in a model quite similar to that employed here. My focus is on all-units discounts rather than RPM, and I consider the cases of lumpy investment and uncertain investment prospects or returns, whereas Romano examined continuous investment returns that are known with certainty. Under Romano's assumptions, two-part tariffs are optimal. Under the assumptions here, more complex tariffs generally dominate two-part tariffs. Romano also does not address entry, which this paper does.

The literature on moral hazard in teams and partnerships[10] identifies conditions under which sharing rules exist that achieve or approximate the first-best outcome in problems with N-sided ($N \geq 2$) moral hazard. This literature developed at a high level of abstraction, and with few exceptions, it does not address the nature of the optimal sharing rules (tariffs) or the relative performance of different rules. Understanding how different sharing rules (tariffs) perform is crucial for developing sensible antitrust policy toward different tariffs and is the main focus of this paper.

Several papers have identified conditions under which penalty schemes can be used to approximate or achieve the first best outcome in *one-sided* moral hazard problems.[11] The use of all-units discounts in this paper is related to the role of penalties in those papers, although here the incentive contract must also deal with the manufacturer's moral hazard. I explain the relationship of my results to this literature as appropriate.

In the first formal analysis of all-units discounts, Kolay et al. (2004) examined their role as a screening device. They found that a price-discriminating monopolist selling to buyers with discrete types does better with all-units discounts than with a menu of self-selecting two-part tariffs. The motivation for all-units discounts here is quite different than it is in their paper. In this paper, there is only one buyer and no hidden information, so monopoly screening is not an issue.

The remainder of this paper is organized as follows. Section II presents the model. Section III examines the deterministic lumpy investment case. Section IV examines the case of uncertain upstream investment prospects and returns. Section V compares all-units discounts and two-block tariffs when the upstream firm faces potential entry, focusing on the case of deterministic returns. Section VI concludes the paper with a discussion of implications, contributions to the literature, and some thoughts on future research.

---

[10]Examples include Holmstrom (1982), Williams & Radner (1988), Legros & Matsushima (1991), and Legros & Matthews (1993).

[11]See, e.g., Mirrlees (1974, 1975, 1999), Gjesdal (1976), Holmstrom (1979, footnote 7), Lewis (1980), and Singh (1984). For a recent example, see Wang (2009).

II. Basic Model

An upstream firm (the "manufacturer") distributes a single product through a downstream firm (the "retailer"). The final demand for the retailer's product is $Q(P, x, I)$, where P is the retail price, I is the manufacturer's investment, and x is the retailer's investment. Assume that Q is decreasing in P and increasing in x and I. For all (x, I), there exists a finite choke price $\overline{P}(x, I)$ above which demand is zero. In the first part of the paper, I assume that demand is known with certainty. Later I consider two types of uncertainty and introduce the additional notation when it is needed.

The investment costs are $m(I)$ for the manufacturer and $r(x)$ for the retailer, both of which are increasing in the levels of investment, with $m(0) = r(0) = 0$. For any levels of investment, the manufacturer and retailer produce at variable costs $C(Q)$ and $V(Q)$, respectively. Variable costs are increasing in Q, with $C(0) = V(0) = 0$. All functions are twice continuously differentiable. To simplify notation in what follows, let $c(Q) = C_Q(Q)$ and $v(Q) = V_Q(Q)$ be the upstream and downstream marginal costs.

Production and contracting are described by a two-stage game. In stage 1, the firms negotiate a supply contract. The contract specifies a fixed fee S that the retailer pays the manufacturer to stock the product (S may be negative, a slotting allowance), and an additional tariff $T(Q)$ that the retailer pays the manufacturer to purchase and resell Q units. This tariff depends on the quantity purchased, but it cannot be conditioned on price or investment levels unless otherwise noted.[12] In stage 2, given the contract terms $(S, T(Q))$, the manufacturer chooses I to maximize its profit, and the retailer simultaneously chooses P and x to maximize its profit. The manufacturer's variable profit is $U = T(Q(P, x, I)) - C(Q(P, x, I)) - m(I)$, and the retailer's variable profit is $\pi = PQ(P, x, I) - V(Q(P, x, I)) - T(Q(P, x, I)) - r(x)$. I look for sub-game perfect equilibria.

The joint profits of the manufacturer and retailer are $\Pi = U + \pi = PQ(P, x, I) - C(Q(P, x, I)) - V(Q(P, x, I)) - m(I) - r(x)$. Let (P^*, x^*, I^*) maximize Π. I will refer to (P^*, I^*, x^*) as the "inte-

---

[12]There are many reasons why price and investment may be non-contractible. For example, RPM may be illegal, or it may be costly for the manufacturer to monitor the retail price. Similarly, it may be difficult for the retailer and/or a court to verify manufacturer and retailer investments.

grated" outcome.

III.   Lumpy Investment with Deterministic Returns

If profits are continuous in own investment and demand is known by both firms at the time of contracting, the equilibrium contract must be continuous at the optimal quantity. If it were discontinuous, either the manufacturer or the retailer could adjust its investment slightly up or down and cause a discrete jump in its profit.[13] In this case, a binding all-units discount tariff—one that induces the retailer to purchase the minimum quantity required to receive a discount—cannot arise in equilibrium.

However, many investments technologies are not continuous. Some investments are lumpy by their nature. Examples include process innovations that enhance quality and discrete marketing projects like participation in trade shows. Even advertising can have a lumpy nature if investment returns are increasing up to a threshold level.[14] Some investments are effectively lumpy due to friction in the business decision-making process. For example, the life cycle of a typical investment project involves a development stage at lower levels within the firm, evaluation by senior management, and an up or down decision on whether to proceed. The investment decision in this context is more about whether to pursue a discrete project proposed to management than it is about minor adjustments of investment levels at the margin.

In this paper, I focus on such lumpy investment:

Assumption 1 (Lumpy Upstream Investment) *The manufacturer chooses investment $I \in \{0, I^*\}$, i.e., it makes the investment I^*, or it invests zero.*

To simplify notation under Assumption 1, let $D(P, x) \equiv Q(P, x, I^*)$ be demand when the upstream firm invests I^*, and let $D^0(P, x) = Q(P, x, 0)$ be demand when it invests zero.

Since the the manufacturer and retailer can exchange a lump sum transfer at the time of contracting, the general contracting problem can be described as choosing a tariff $T(\cdot)$, retail price

---

[13]See Romano (2004).

[14]A large marketing literature documents and explores the implications of S-shaped advertising return functions that are convex over advertising levels below an inflection point. See, e.g., Dube et al. (2005), Vakratsas et al (2004), and the references cited therein. Researchers in this literature have argued that S-shaped advertising returns can explain advertising "pulsing," whereby firms switch advertising on and off over time.

P, and investment levels x and I to maximize joint profits subject to the constraints that I and (P, x) are mutual best responses for the manufacturer and retailer given $T(\cdot)$. If the firms choose not to induce upstream investment, only the retailer's incentives matter, and joint profits can be maximized (conditional on no upstream investment) with a two-part tariff that makes the retailer the residual claimant to joint profits. There is no role for more complex contracts. The more interesting case examined in this paper is when firms decide to induce upstream investment. In this case, the optimal contract solves the "general contracting problem:"

$$\text{(GCP)} \quad \max_{P, x, T(\cdot) \in \mathcal{T}} \Pi = PD(P, x) - C(D(P, x)) - V(D(P, x)) - r(x) - m(I^*) \ \ s.t.$$

$$\text{(1)} \qquad (P, x) = \arg\max_{(P', x')} P'D(P', x') - V(D(P', x')) - T(D(P', x')) - r(x'),$$

$$\text{(2)} \qquad T(D(P, x)) - C(D(P, x)) - m(I^*) \geq T(D^0(P, x)) - C(D^0(P, x)).$$

where $\mathcal{T}$ is the set of all feasible contracts.

Before addressing the general contracting problem directly (see subsection III.B below), I begin by comparing three simple, commonly-observed tariffs: two-part tariffs (TP), declining block tariffs with two blocks (TB), and all-units discounts with two prices (TA). These tariffs are written as follows:

$$T^{TP}(Q) = \begin{cases} 0 & \text{if } Q = 0, \\ F + wQ & \text{if } Q > 0, \end{cases}$$

$$T^{TB}(Q) = \begin{cases} 0 & \text{if } Q = 0, \\ F + w_1 Q & \text{if } 0 < Q < q, \\ F + w_2 Q + (w_1 - w_2)q & \text{if } Q \geq q, \end{cases}$$

$$T^{TA}(Q) = \begin{cases} w_1 Q & \text{if } 0 \leq Q < q, \\ w_2 Q & \text{if } Q \geq q \end{cases}$$

where w, w_1, and w_2 are wholesale prices, F is a fixed fee, and q is a quantity threshold that determines the applicable per-unit price.[15]

The two-part tariff is the standard "continuous" tariff[16] that appears in much of the literature on vertical control. The two-block tariff is a slightly more flexible continuous tariff, charging two

---

[15] Of course, T^{TB} and T^{TA} only exhibit marginal price "discounts" if $w_2 < w_1$.

[16] It is continuous except at zero.

different marginal prices depending on whether quantity falls in the first block ($Q < q$) or second block ($Q \geq q$). In most of the literature on vertical control, customer-specific two-block tariffs are equivalent to customer-specific two-part tariffs, because a customer purchasing in the second block will view the extra payment $(w_1 - w_2)q$ for quantities in the first block as part of the fixed fee. The all-units discount tariff is similar to the two-block tariff in that it specifies two prices that depend on whether the quantity purchased is above and below a quantity threshold q. However it differs in two key respects: (1) customers that purchase in the second block ($Q \geq q$) do not pay an implicit fixed fee; and (2) if $w_1 > w_2$, the all-units discount tariff is discontinuous at q. As I have noted, all-units discounts have received little formal attention in the literature on vertical control.[17]

The following preliminary result motivates the potential role for all-units discounts and two-block tariffs in this model.

Proposition 1 *Two-part tariffs support the integrated outcome if and only if the manufacturer's incremental quasi-rents from investment at wholesale price $w^* = D(P^*, x^*)$ are sufficiently large.*

Proof: Under a two-part tariff, the retailer will choose the fully integrated price and investment only if it faces the same marginal incentives as an integrated firm. This requires the wholesale price $w^* = c(D(P^*, x^*))$. The upstream firm's incremental profit from investing is then

$$(3) \qquad \Delta = \int_{D^0(P^*, x^*)}^{D(P^*, x^*)} [w^* - c(q)] dq - m(I^*)$$

The integral represents the manufacturer's incremental quasi-rents from investment at the wholesale price w^*. The integrated outcome is supported if and only if $\Delta \geq 0$, which requires sufficiently large quasi-rents. **Q.E.D.**

Proposition 1 is the lumpy investment analog of Proposition 1 in Romano (2004), which established that two-part tariffs cannot support the integrated outcome when the manufacturer chooses investment from a continuous set.[18] In the remainder of this paper, I assume that the manufacturer produces at constant marginal cost c (no quasi-rents). This rules out the possible efficiency of two-

---

[17]Kolay et al. (2004) is the primary exception.

[18]Although he assumed constant marginal cost, a two-part tariff would not support the integrated outcome in his model even with high quasi-rents because the manufacturer would distort its continuous investment choice at the margin.

part tariffs due to manufacturer quasi-rents, focusing attention on cases in which more complex contracts might do better.

A. Optimal All-Units Discounts

Next I characterize the optimal all-units discount tariff. Define an *effective* all-units discount as one in which $w_1 > w_2$, and the retailer elects to sell enough to reach the discount threshold q and pay the lower price w_2. (An ineffective all-units discount would have the same incentive effects as a two-part tariff with wholesale price w_1.) Under an effective all-units discount that induces upstream investment, there are three constraints on the firms' investment and pricing decisions. First, the retailer will choose P and x to maximize its profit given the all-units discount quantity threshold:

$$(4) \qquad (P, x) = \arg\max_{(P', x')} \ (P' - w_2)D(P', x') - V(D(P', x')) - r(x') \ \ s.t. \ \ D(P', x') \geq q.$$

Second, the retailer must earn more by selling at least q units at price w_2 than by "defecting" from the all-units discount and optimizing against the higher wholesale price w_1:

$$(5) \ \ (P - w_2)D(P, x) - V(D(P, x)) - r(x) \geq \hat{\pi}(w_1) \equiv \max_{(P', x')} \ (P' - w_1)D(P', x') - V(D(P', x')) - r(x').$$

Third, the manufacturer must find it profitable to invest:

$$(6) \qquad\qquad\qquad (w_2 - c)D(P, x) - m(I^*) \geq \hat{U}$$

where $\hat{U}$ is the profit the manufacturer earns if it "defects" by choosing not to invest. This profit is

$$\hat{U} = \begin{cases} (w_1 - c)D^0(P, x) & \text{if } D^0(P, x) < q, \\ (w_2 - c)D^0(P, x) & \text{if } D^0(P, x) \geq q. \end{cases}$$

The optimal all-units discount maximizes joint profits Π subject to (4), (5), and (6).

The following assumption simplifies the analysis.

Assumption 2 *(First Order Sufficiency) The first order conditions to the maximization problem in (4) are sufficient for (P, x) to solve (4).*

Assumption 2 holds if π is concave and $D(P,x)$ is quasiconcave, though it may also hold with weaker conditions on demand.

Given Assumption 2, an effective all-units discount that induces upstream investment will solve

$$\text{(AUDT)} \quad \max_{(P,x,w_1,w_2,q,\xi)} (P-c)D(P,x) - V(D(P,x)) - r(x) - m(I^*) \quad s.t.$$

(7) $$(P - w_2)D(P,x) - V(D(P,x)) - r(x) \geq \hat{\pi}(w_1),$$

(8) $$(w_2 - c)D(P,x) - m(I^*) \geq \hat{U},$$

(9) $$D(P,x) + (P - v(D(P,x)) - w_2)D_P(P,x) + \xi D_P(P,x) = 0,$$

(10) $$(P - v(D(P,x)) - w_2)D_x(P,x) - r_x(x) + \xi D_x(P,x) = 0,$$

(11) $$D(P,x) \geq q,$$

(12) $$\xi(D(P,x) - q) = 0$$

where conditions (9) through (12) are the first order conditions for (P,x) to maximize the retailer's profit, and ξ is the Lagrangian multiplier in the retailer's program (4). The Lagrangian for (AUDT) is[19]

$$\mathcal{L} = (P-c)D - V - r - m + \lambda[(P-w_2)D - V - r - \hat{\pi}] + \eta[(w_2-c)D - m - \hat{U}]$$
$$+ \gamma_1[D + (P - v - w_2 + \xi)D_P] + \gamma_2[(P - v - w_2 + \xi)D_x - r_x] + \gamma_3[D - q] + \gamma_4\xi[D - q].$$

The following lemmas characterize the role of the quantity constraint in the all-units discount.

Lemma 1 *In any effective all-units discount that improves upon a two-part tariff, $q \geq D^0(P,x)$, and thus $\hat{U} = (w_1 - c)D^0(P,x)$.*

Proof: Suppose $q < D^0(P,x)$. Then $\xi = 0$, and the quantity constraint does not affect the manufacturer's investment decision. It is then optimal to set w_1 arbitrarily high to relax (7) as much as possible, which sets $\hat{\pi}(w_1) = 0$. The contracting problem is then equivalent to choosing a two-part tariff with fixed fee S and wholesale price w_2. **Q.E.D.**

---

[19]Arguments of functions are omitted for brevity except when this could cause confusion.

Lemma 2 *In characterizing the optimal retail price and investment levels under an all-units discount that improves upon two-part tariffs, there is no loss of generality in considering only cases in which (11) is binding (i.e., $D(P, x) = q$).*

Proof: Suppose constraint (11) does not bind. Then $\gamma_3 = 0$, and since the constraint in the retailer's optimization problem is slack, $\xi = 0$. The derivative of the Lagrangian with respect to q is then $\mathcal{L}_q = -\gamma_3 - \gamma_4 \xi = 0$, and the other derivatives of the Lagrangian do not depend on q. Therefore increasing q until $q = D(P, x)$ does not affect the maximized joint profits or the optimal investment levels. **Q.E.D.**

Using $D(P, x) = q$ and $\hat{U} = (w_1 - c)D^0(P, x)$ from Lemmas 1 and 2, the first order conditions for w_1, w_2, and ξ are

$$(13) \qquad \mathcal{L}_{w_1} = -\lambda \hat{\pi}_{w_1} - \eta D^0(P, x) = 0,$$

$$(14) \qquad \mathcal{L}_{w_2} = -(\lambda - \eta)D - \gamma_1 D_P - \gamma_2 D_x = 0,$$

$$(15) \qquad \mathcal{L}_{\xi} = \gamma_1 D_P + \gamma_2 D_x = 0.$$

Substituting $\mathcal{L}_{\xi}$ into $\mathcal{L}_{w_2}$ implies $\lambda = \eta$. So the constraints (7) and (8) are either both binding or both slack. If the constraints are binding, substituting $\lambda = \eta$ into $\mathcal{L}_{w_1}$ and applying the envelope theorem yields

$$(16) \qquad -\hat{\pi}_{w_1}(\hat{P}(w_1), \hat{x}(w_1)) = D(\hat{P}(w_1), \hat{x}(w_1)) = D^0(P, x)$$

where $(\hat{P}(w_1), \hat{x}(w_1)) = \arg\max_{P', x'}(P' - w_1)D(P', x') - V(D(P', x')) - r(x')$.

Condition (16) has an intuitive interpretation that illuminates the key factors in play in the double moral hazard problem with lumpy investment. To see this, add constraints (7) and (8) to get

$$(17) \qquad m(I^*) \leq (P - c)D(P, x) - V(D(P, x)) - r(x) - \left[\hat{\pi}(w_1) + (w_1 - c)D^0(P, x).\right]$$

The bracketed term in (17) is sum of (i) the retailer's profit if it defects by choosing output too low to receive the discount and optimizes against w_1; and (ii) the manufacturer's profit if it defects by choosing not to invest. The highest upstream investment cost such that all-units discounts can support (P, x) in equilibrium is found by choosing w_1 to minimize the sum of the defection profits. The minimum occurs where $D(\hat{P}(w_1), \hat{x}(w_1)) = D^0(P, x)$, as in (16).

To determine whether all units discounts can support the integrated outcome, fix the retail price and investment at their integrated levels, (P^*, x^*). For any given wholesale price w_2 in the low price tier, the retailer incentive constraints (9) and (10) can be satisfied by choosing ξ so that $w_2 - \xi = c$. This gives the retailer the same effective marginal cost (including the shadow cost ξ) as an integrated firm. All-units discounts will support the integrated outcome if there exist values of w_1 and w_2 that also satisfy constraints (7) and (8) when evaluated at (P^*, x^*).

Let $w_2^R(w_1)$ be the value of w_2 that solves the retailer's participation constraint (7) with equality. That is, $w_2^R(w_1)$ is the retailer's iso-profit contour representing the set of wholesale prices over which it is just indifferent between pricing and investing to reach the discount threshold q and defecting by optimizing against w_1. Similarly let $w_2^M(w_1)$ solve the manufacturer's participation constraint (8) with equality; $w_2^M(w_1)$ is the manufacturer's iso-profit contour along which it is just indifferent between investing I^* and investing zero. Using these definitions, the participation constraints (7) and (8) can be rewritten as

$$(18) \qquad w_2 \leq w_2^R(w_1) = \frac{P^* D(P^*, x^*) - V(D(P^*, x^*)) - r(x^*) - \hat{\pi}(w_1)}{D(P^*, x^*)},$$

$$(19) \qquad w_2 \geq w_2^M(w_1) = \frac{w_1 D^0(P^*, x^*) + m(I^*) + c[D(P^*, x^*) - D^0(P^*, x^*)]}{D(P^*, x^*)}.$$

Let $\overline{w}_1$ be the wholesale price that induces the retail choke price in the event the retailer defects. That is, i.e., $D(\hat{P}(\overline{w}_1), \hat{x}(\overline{w}_1)) = 0$. The functions $w_2^R(w_1)$ are $w_2^M(w_1)$ are plotted in Figure 1 using the following facts, which are easy to confirm:

$$w_2^R(c) = c, \qquad \frac{\partial w_2^R(c)}{\partial w_1} = \frac{-\hat{\pi}_{w_1}(c)}{D(P^*, x^*)} = \frac{D(\hat{P}(c), \hat{x}(c))}{D(P^*, x^*)} = 1, \qquad \frac{\partial w_2^R(\overline{w}_1)}{\partial w_1} = 0,$$

$$w_2^M(c) = c + \frac{m(I^*)}{D(P^*, x^*)}, \qquad \frac{\partial w_1^M(w_1)}{\partial w_1} = \frac{D^0(P^*, x^*)}{D(P^*, x^*)} < 1 \; \forall \; w_1.$$

The retailer's iso-profit contour intersects the point $(w_1, w_2) = (c, c)$ with a slope of one. The

13

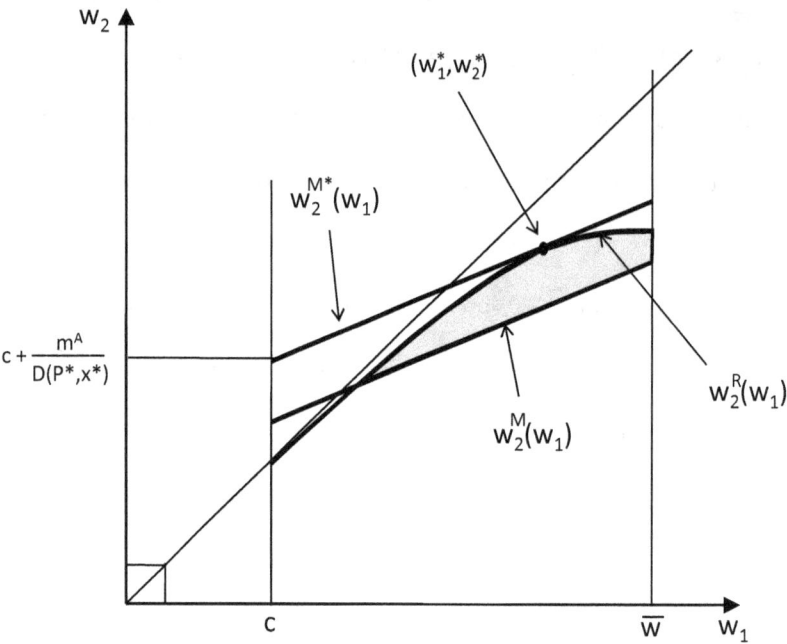

Figure 1: Equilibrium wholesale prices under all-units discounts.

manufacturer's iso-profit contour crosses the line $w_1 = c$ above the retailer's by an amount equal to $m(I^*)/D(P^*, x^*)$ and with a slope less than one. It follows that if the upstream investment cost $m(I^*)$ is sufficiently small, there exist wholesale prices (w_1, w_2) such $w_2 \leq w_2^R(w_1)$ and $w_2 \geq w_2^M(w_1)$. These are the prices that lie in the shaded area in Figure 1 (the value m^A is defined in Proposition 2 below). This proves the following proposition.

Proposition 2 *Under lumpy investment with deterministic returns, there exists an upstream investment cost threshold m^A such that, for all investment costs below m^A, a two-price all-units discount supports the integrated outcome.*

The highest investment cost such that all-units discounts support the integrated outcome is represented geometrically in Figure 1 as the investment cost associated with the point of tangency between the iso profit contours. This can be found by solving

$$\max_{w_1, w_2} m(I^*) = (w_2 - c)D(P^*, x^*) - (w_1 - c)D^0(P^*, x^*)$$

(20)
$$s.t. \ (P - w_2)D(P^*, x^*) - V(D(P^*, x^*)) - r(x^*) - \pi(w_1) \geq 0.$$

14

It is straightforward to confirm that the solution yields condition (16). That is, minimizing the sum of the defection profits allows all-units discounts to support upstream investment for the highest possible investment costs.

Analytically, m^A is the right hand side of (17) evaluated at (P^*, x^*). Using condition (16), m^A can be written

$$m^A = \{(P^* - c)D(P^*, x^*) - V(D(P^*, x^*)) - r(x^*)\} - \left\{(\hat{P} - c)D^0(P^*, x^*) - V(D^0(P^*, x^*)) - r(\hat{x})\right\}.$$

Let m^* be the maximum upstream investment a fully integrated firm would make. This is

$$m^* = \{(P^* - c)D(P^*, x^*) - V(D(P^*, x^*)) - r(x^*)\} - \left\{\max_{P,x}(P - c)D^0(P, x) - V(D^0(P, x)) - r(x)\right\}.$$

Subtracting m^A from m^* gives

$$m^* - m^A = \left\{(\hat{P} - c)D^0(P^*, x^*) - V(D^0(P^*, x^*)) - r(\hat{x})\right\} - \left\{\max_{P,x}(P - c)D^0(P, x) - V(D^0(P, x)) - r(x)\right\}.$$

If $m^* - m^A > 0$, an integrated firm would make investments that cannot be supported by all-units discounts.

A simple example shows that $m^* - m^A$ may be positive, which means that all-units discounts may not support the integrated outcome. Suppose demand is unaffected by downstream investment (fix x at zero), assume $V_Q = v$ is constant, and let $D^0(P, 0) = \alpha D(P, 0)$ for some $\alpha < 1$. Then the integrated price P^* also maximizes joint profit when there is no upstream investment. The difference between m^* and m^A is then

$$(\hat{P} - c - v)D^0(P^*, 0) - (P^* - c - v)D^0(P^*, 0) > 0,$$

since $\hat{P} > P^*$.

A remaining question is whether all-units discounts improve upon two-part tariffs whenever they support upstream investment. The following assumption is required to establish this.

Assumption 3 $D(\hat{P}(w_1), \hat{x}(w_1))$ *is decreasing in* w_1.

Assumption 3 is the standard case, but it is not guaranteed by the other assumptions. It holds if the cross partials of D are not too large. It implies that the retailer's defection profit $\hat{\pi}(w_1)$ is convex and the retailer's iso-profit contour $w_2^R(w_1)$ is concave in w_1. The curve $w_2^R(w_1)$ is drawn this way in Figure 1, although Assumption 3 is not required for Proposition 2.

Proposition 3 *Suppose Assumption 3 holds. Under lumpy investment with deterministic returns, if all units discounts support upstream investment, they yield higher joint profits than two-part tariffs.*

Proof: Note that the general character of Figure 1 does not change when the iso-profit contours are evaluated at any $(P, x) \neq (P^*, x^*)$. In particular, the manufacturer's iso-profit contour has a slope between zero and one, while the slope of the the retailer's iso-profit contour runs from one to zero as w_1 runs between c and $\overline{w}_1$. The wholesale prices in the optimal all-units discount occur at a point of tangency between w_2^M and w_2^R. Since $w_2^R(w_1)$ is concave by Assumption 3, the point of tangency yields $w_2 < w_1$. This tariff dominates any two-part tariff, since the firms could have chosen $w_1 = w_2$. **Q.E.D**

B.   All-units Discounts are Optimal Contracts

I return now to the general contracting problem (GCP) introduced at the beginning of this section. Let $(P^e, x^e, T^e(\cdot))$ solve (GCP), and let $(P^A, x^A, w_1^A, w_2^A, q^A)$ solve (AUDT).

Proposition 4 *Under lumpy investment with deterministic returns, a two-price all-units discount is an optimal contract, i.e., $(P^A, x^A) = (P^e, x^e)$.*

Proof: Recall that $T^e(\cdot)$ is chosen from the set of all feasible contracts, $\mathcal{T}$. Let $\mathcal{F} \subset \mathcal{T}$ be the set of all two-point forcing contacts of the form

$$T^F(Q) = \begin{cases} T_1 & \text{if } Q = D^0(P', x') \\ T_2 & \text{if } Q = D(P', x') \\ \infty & \text{otherwise.} \end{cases}$$

The method of proof is to show that (GCP) can be solved by restricting attention to contracts from the set $\mathcal{F}$, and that the solution to (AUDT) yields the same price and investment levels as when contracts from the set $\mathcal{F}$ are employed.

Consider the specific two-point forcing contract

$$T^{Fe}(Q) = \begin{cases} T^e(D^0(P^e, x^e)) & \text{if } Q = D^0(P^e, x^e) \\ T^e(D(P^e, x^e)) & \text{if } Q = D(P^e, x^e) \\ \infty & \text{otherwise.} \end{cases}$$

Under this contract, the retailer will choose either (P^e, x^e), or some (P', x') such that $D(P', x') = D^0(P^e, x^e)$. Any other choice would be unprofitable. Since (P^e, x^e, T^e) solves (GCP), it follows that for all (P', x'),

$$P^e D(P^e, x^e) - V(D(P^e, x^e)) - T^{Fe}(D(P^e, x^e)) - r(x^e)$$

$$= P^e D(P^e, x^e) - V(D(P^e, x^e)) - T^e(D(P^e, x^e)) - r(x^e)$$

$$(21) \qquad \geq P'D(P', x') - V(D(P', x')) - T^e(D(P', x')) - r(x').$$

Since (21) is true for all (P', x'), it is also true for any (P', x') such that $D(P', x') = D^0(P^e, x^e)$. Therefore, for all (P', x') such that $D(P', x') = D^0(P^e, x^e)$,

$$P^e D(P^e, x^e) - V(D(P^e, x^e)) - T^{Fe}(D(P^e, x^e)) - r(x^e)$$

$$\geq P'D^0(P^e, x^e) - V(D^0(P^e, x^e)) - T^e(D^0(P^e, x^e)) - r(x')$$

$$(22) \qquad = P'D^0(P^e, x^e) - V(D^0(P^e, x^e)) - T^{Fe}(D^0(P^e, x^e)) - r(x').$$

This implies that the retailer optimality constraint (1) is satisfied at (P^e, x^e) under $T^{Fe}(\cdot)$. Similarly, by the definition of (P^e, x^e, T^e),

$$T^{Fe}(D(P^e, x^e)) - cD(P^e, x^e) - m(I^*) = T^e(D(P^e, x^e)) - cD(P^e, x^e) - m(I^*)$$

$$\geq T^e(D^0(P^e, x^e)) - cD^0(P^e, x^e)$$

$$= T^{Fe}(D^0(P^e, x^e)) - cD^0(P^e, x^e),$$

which means the manufacturer's optimality constraint (2) is also satisfied at (P^e, x^e) under $T^{Fe}(\cdot)$. Therefore, the two-point forcing contract $T^{Fe}(\cdot)$ solves (GCP).

Next I argue that the solution to (AUDT) can also be characterized by the same two-point forcing contract. Under the optimal all-units discount, $D(\hat{P}(w_1^A), \hat{x}(w_1^A)) = D^0(P^A, x^A)$ by (16). Therefore, the retailer's decision whether to price and invest as expected under the all-units discount or optimize against w_1^A is effectively a decision whether to produce $D(P^A, x^A)$ or $D^0(P^A, x^A)$. The manufacturer is effectively choosing between the same two points. Thus, there is no loss of generality in restricting attention to two-point forcing contracts of the form

$$T^{FA}(Q) = \begin{cases} w_1 D^0(P', x') & \text{if } Q = D^0(P', x') \\ w_2 D(P', x') & \text{if } Q = D(P', x') \\ \infty & \text{otherwise.} \end{cases}$$

Note that T^{FA} takes the same form as T^{Fe}, with $w_1 D^0(P', x') = T_1$ and $w_2 D(P', x') = T_2$. Since the optimal contract and the optimal all-units discount can both be characterized using two-point forcing contracts, they yield the same outcome. **Q.E.D.**

The use of all-units discounts in this model bears a close relationship to the use of quantity forcing to eliminate double marginalization. In addressing double marginalization, there is no loss of generality in restricting attention to a single point forcing contract that specifies one price for the efficient quantity and an infinite price (or any price above the choke price) for any other quantity. It happens that a traditional forcing contract, which specifies one price for quantities that equal or exceed the efficient quantity and an infinite (or very high) price for quantities below the efficient level can achieve the same outcome as a single point forcing contract, because quantities greater than the efficient quantity are dominated under such a contract. Here, a single point forcing contract would also be sufficient if the manufacturer did not make an investment decision. However, because the manufacturer can choose not to invest, the contract must specify prices for two points, D and D^0, and the prices must be set so that choosing D dominates choosing D^0 for both the manufacturer and the retailer. It happens that an all-units discount can support the same outcome as a two-point forcing contract, because under the optimal all-units discount, choices other than D and D^0 are dominated.

C. Two-Block Tariffs

All-units discounts work by offering an incentive that lowers the retailer's shadow cost of producing output to $w_2^A - \xi + v$, while keeping the wholesale price w_2^A high enough to compensate the manufacturer for investment. One might conjecture that a continuous tariff, say a declining block tariff, might accomplish the same objective with a wholesale price in the low-price block equal to

$w_2^A - \xi$ and an inframarginal price in the high-price block that compensates the manufacturer for investing. I now show that this conjecture is correct when investment returns are deterministic.

Define an *effective* two-block tariff as one in which the retailer purchases in the low-price block and pays the marginal price w_2. A two-block tariff that supports upstream investment I^* will solve

$$(\text{TBT}) \quad \max_{(P,x,w_1,w_2,q)} (P-c)D(P,x) - V(D(P,x)) - r(x) - m(I^*) \quad s.t.$$

(23)
$$(P - w_2)D(P,x) - V(D(P,x)) - (w_1 - w_2)q - r(x) \geq \hat{\pi}(w_1),$$

(24)
$$(w_2 - c)D(P,x) + (w_1 - w_2)q - m(I^*) \geq U^{DT},$$

(25)
$$D(P,x) + (P - v(D(P,x)) - w_2)D_P(P,x) = 0,$$

(26)
$$(P - v(D(P,x)) - w_2)D_x(P,x) - r_x(x) = 0,$$

(27)
$$D(P,q) \geq q$$

where

$$U^{DT} = \begin{cases} (w_1 - c)D^0(P,x) & \text{if } D^0(P,x) \leq q, \\ (w_2 - c)D^0(P,x) + (w_1 - w_2)q & \text{if } D^0(P,x) > q. \end{cases}$$

The Lagrangian is

$$\begin{aligned} \mathcal{L}^T &= (P-c)D - V - r - m + \lambda[(P - w_2)D - V - (w_1 - w_2)q - r - \hat{\pi}] \\ &\quad + \eta[(w_2 - c)D + (w_1 - w_2)q - m - U^{DT}] \\ &\quad + \gamma_1[D + (P - v - w_2)D_P] + \gamma_2[(P - v - w_2)D_x - r_x] + \gamma_3[D - q]. \end{aligned}$$

Lemma 3 *In characterizing the optimal retail price and investment levels under an effective two-block tariff, there is no loss of generality from considering only cases in which $q \geq D^0(P,x)$, and thus $U^{DT} = (w_1 - c)D^0(P,x)$.*

Proof: Suppose $q < D^0(P,x)$, so that $U^{DT} = (w_2 - c)D^0(P,x) + (w_1 - w_2)q$. Constraint (27) is then slack, since $q < D^0(P,x) < D(P,x)$, and q does not enter constraints (25) and (26). The first order condition with respect to q is $\mathcal{L}_q^T = -\lambda(w_1 - w_2) = 0$. Since $w_1 > w_2$ for any effective two-block tariff, this implies that $\lambda = 0$, which means that constraint (23) is slack. Thus, raising q to $D^0(P,x)$ affects the constraint set only by relaxing constraint (24), which either increases joint profits or, if (24) is not binding, leaves both joint profits and the optimal investment levels unchanged. **Q.E.D**

Proposition 5 *Under lumpy investment and deterministic returns, two-block tariffs and all-units discounts are equivalent tariffs. Both are optimal contracts.*

Proof: Let $(P^A, x^A, w_1^A, w_2^A, q^A, \xi^A)$ solve (AUDT). I will show that there exists a vector (w_1, w_2, q) such that constraints (23) through (27) are satisfied when evaluated at (P^A, x^A). This means that (P^A, x^A) is feasible under two-block tariffs, and since two-block tariffs cannot do better than all-units discount tariffs (by Proposition 3), two block tariffs will yield the same outcome as all-units discounts.

Let $w_2 = w_2^A - \xi^A$ and $w_1 = w_1^A$. Constraints (25) and (26) are then identical to (9) and (10) and are therefore satisfied. Constraints (23) and (24) (using Lemma 3) can be written

(28) $(P^A - w_2^A)D(P^A, x^A) - V(D(P^A, x^A)) - r(x^A) + \{\xi^A[D(P^A, x^A) - q] - (w_1^A - w_2^A)q\} \geq \hat{\pi}(w_1^A),$

(29) $(w_2^A - c)D(P^A, x^A) - m(I^*) - \{\xi^A[D(P^A, x^A) - q] - (w_1^A - w_2^A)q\} \geq (w_1^A - c)D^0(P^A, x^A).$

Constraints (28) and (29) are identical to (7) and (8) except for the term in curly braces. These conditions will be satisfied if the term in curly braces equals zero, which is true when

(30) $$q = \frac{\xi^A}{w_1^A - w_2^A + \xi^A} D(P^A, x^A).$$

Choosing q to satisfy (30) is feasible. Thus, constraints (23) through (27) are satisfied when evaluated at (P^A, x^A), and two block tariffs yield the same outcome as all-units discounts. **Q.E.D**

The equivalence between all-units discounts and two-block tariffs in the perfect certainty case is not especially surprising given the intuition following Proposition 3. Just as a tariff with a single marginal price can replicate a one-point forcing contract for the case in which only retail incentives matter, a two-block tariff with two marginal prices can replicate a two-point forcing contract for the case in which both retail and manufacturer incentives matter.

IV.   Uncertain Investment Prospects and Returns

The previous section established the equivalence of two-price all-units discounts and two-block tariffs when upstream investment is lumpy and investment returns are certain. In this section,

20

I introduce two notions of uncertainty in the lumpy investment model[20] and show that all-units discounts and declining block tariffs are no longer equivalent. The two cases are described as follows:

Definition 1 (Uncertain Prospects). *At the time of contracting, firms are uncertain whether a productive upstream investment project exists. The prospects for investment are revealed to the manufacturer before its investment decision, but after contracts have been signed.*

Definition 2 (Uncertain Returns). *The random returns from investment are unknown to both the manufacturer and the retailer at the time of contracting.*

The case of uncertain prospects might arise if the manufacturer is engaged in ongoing research that randomly yields productive investment projects during the period covered by the contract. Uncertain returns is the standard case that appears in most of the agency literature where investment yields a noisy return.[21]

Assume that firms have prior beliefs that investment I^* will yield demand $D(P, x)$ with probability θ and demand $D^0(P, x)$ with probability $1 - \theta$. For the case of uncertain prospects, θ is the probability that an upstream investment project becomes available to the manufacturer that would increase demand from D^0 to D. For the case of uncertain returns, θ is the probability that investment will increase demand from D^0 to D.

The contracting game is similar to that in the previous section, except that investment returns are uncertain when contracts are signed. In stage one, firms negotiate $(S, T(\cdot))$. In stage two, the manufacturer decides whether to invest zero or I^*, and the retailer simultaneously chooses P and x. Uncertain prospects and returns differ according to whether the manufacturer knows whether a productive investment opportunity exists before making its investment decision.

In either case, the best firms can hope to achieve without integrating is to maximize joint profits conditional on P and x being chosen before the resolution of uncertainty. Let (P^*, x^*, I^*) be this

---

[20] The lumpy investment assumption is retained for consistency with the previous section and because it is sufficient to establish the main points of the paper. I discuss the effects of relaxing this assumption in Section VI.

[21] A third case of interest is when the manufacturer has private information about investment returns when contracts are signed. In this case, which I have not analyzed, the contract would have elements of signalling and screening.

"first best" outcome.[22] In both cases I assume that investing I^* is jointly optimal. The optimal retail price and investment solve

$$(31) \qquad \max_{P,x} \ (P-c)\overline{D}(P,x) - \theta V(D(P,x)) - (1-\theta)V(D^0(P,x)) - m(I^*) - r(x)$$

where $\overline{D}(P,x) = \theta D(P,x) + (1-\theta)D^0(P,x)$ is the expected quantity if the manufacturer plans to invest under uncertain prospects or chooses to invest under uncertain returns.

A. Sufficient Conditions for All-Units Discounts to Support the First Best Outcome

Two special cases are of interest.

Case 1 (No Downstream Investment Returns). $D^0(P,x) = D^0(P,0)$ and $D(P,x) = D(P,0) \ \forall x$.

Case 2 (Iso-Elastic Upstream Investment). $D^0(P,x) = \alpha D(P,x)$ for some $\alpha \in (0,1)$.

In Case 1, the retailer's only decision is its choice of price. This is equivalent to assuming that the manufacturer and retailer can contract directly over downstream investment so that the retailer does not make an independent investment choice. Note that this assumption does *not* trivialize the problem, as the downstream firm's pricing decision is still susceptible to double-marginalization. Technically, the problem still involves double-moral hazard, but the retailer's moral hazard has a single dimension (only price) rather than two (price and investment). In Case 2, upstream investment produces an iso-elastic shift in demand that does not affect the elasticities of demand with respect of P and x.

Let $a(P,x)$ be the retailer's average incremental cost of expanding output from $D^0(P,x)$ to $D(P,x)$:

$$(32) \qquad a(P,x) = \frac{V(D(P,x)) - V(D^0(P,x))}{D(P,x) - D^0(P,x)}.$$

Let $a^* = a(P^*, x^*)$ be the average incremental cost at the first best retail price and investment levels. The following proposition provides sufficient conditions for all-units discounts to achieve the first best outcome.

---

[22]I am following much of the literature in referring to the optimal outcome conditional given the information constraints as the "first best."

Proposition 6 *Under uncertain prospects or returns:*

1. *If the retailer's only decision is price (Case 1), then a two-price all-units discount supports the first best outcome.*

2. *Suppose upstream investment causes an iso-elastic shift in demand (Case 2).*

    (a) *If $\int_0^{D^0(P^*,x^*)}[a^* - v(q)]dq \geq r(x^*)$, then a two-price all-units discount supports the first best outcome.*

    (b) *If $\int_0^{D^0(P^*,x^*)}[a^* - v(q)]dq < r(x^*)$, then an all-units discount with a minimum commitment and penalty for breach supports the first best outcome.*

3. *Two-block tariffs do not support the first best outcome for all parameter values in Cases 1 and 2.*

Proof:

Parts 1 and 2. I first show by construction that all-units discounts support the first best outcome in Cases 1 and 2. Consider the following two-price all-units discount with a minimum commitment of $\overline{Q}$ and penalty for breach of K:

$$T^*(Q) = \begin{cases} K + w_1 Q & \text{if } Q < \overline{Q}, \\ w_1 Q & \text{if } \overline{Q} \leq Q < D^0(P^*, x^*), \\ w_2 Q & \text{if } Q \geq D^0(P^*, x^*). \end{cases}$$

If K and w_1 are sufficiently large, a retailer governed by T^* will choose (P, x) to ensure that its sales are at least $D^0(P^*, x^*)$ *in all states of the world*. That is, it will maximize its expected profits subject to $D^0(P, x) \geq D^0(P^*, x^*)$. Note that this is true under both uncertain prospects and returns. Suppose the contract specifies K and w_1 high enough to induce this behavior. (Below I determine whether $K > 0$ is actually required and discuss how high w_1 must be.) Then the optimal contract of the form T^* solves

(AUDT-U) $\quad \max_{(P,x,w_2,q,\xi)} (P - c)\overline{D}(P, x) - \theta V(D(P, x)) - (1 - \theta)V(D^0(P, x)) - r(x) - m(I^*)$ *s.t.*

(33)
$$(w_2 - c)D - m \geq (w_2 - c)D^0 \quad \text{(Uncertain Prospects)}$$
$$(w_2 - c)\overline{D} - m \geq (w_2 - c)D^0 \quad \text{(Uncertain Returns)},$$

23

(34) $$\overline{D} + (P - w_2)\overline{D}_P - \theta v(D)D_P - (1-\theta)v(D^0)D_P^0 + \xi D_P^0 = 0,$$

(35) $$(P - w_2)\overline{D}_x - \theta v(D)D_x - (1-\theta)v(D^0)D_x^0 - r_x + \xi D_x^0 = 0,$$

(36) $$D^0(P, x) \geq D^0(P^*, x^*),$$

(37) $$\xi[D^0(P, x) - D^0(P^*, x^*)] = 0$$

where ξ is again the Lagrangian multiplier in the retailer's optimization problem. Note that only one of the constraints in (33) must be satisfied, depending on whether the uncertainty is over prospects or returns. Set $P = P^*$, $x = x^*$, $w_2 = P^* - a^*$, and

$$\xi = \frac{(P^* - c - a^*)\overline{D}_P(P^*, x^*)}{D_P^0(P^*, x^*)}.$$

Substituting into conditions (33) through (37) shows that (36) and (37) are satisfied trivially. After some algebra, and using $D^0 = \alpha D$ (Case 2), (33) through (35) become

(38)
$$(P^* - c)[D - D^0] - [V(D) - V(D^0)] \geq m \qquad \text{(Uncertain Prospects)}$$
$$(P^* - c)[\overline{D} - D^0] - [\theta V(D) + (1-\theta)V(D^0) - V(D^0)] \geq m \qquad \text{(Uncertain Returns)},$$

(39) $$\overline{D} + (P - c)\overline{D}_P - \theta v(D)D_P - (1-\theta)v(D^0)D_P^0 = 0,$$

(40) $$(P - c)\overline{D}_x - \theta v(D)D_x - (1-\theta)v(D^0)D_x^0 - r_x = 0.$$

The conditions in (38) are the same as the conditions under which an integrated manufacturer would invest I^* under uncertain prospects and returns. Conditions (39) and (40) are the same as the first order conditions for the first best problem (31). Therefore, the first best retail price and investment satisfy (33) through (35). This establishes that all-units discounts with a minimum commitment and sufficiently high penalty for breach achieve the first best outcome in Case 2. In Case 1, condition (35) is irrelevant, and it is straightforward to show that the same substitutions establish that the other constraints hold.

Whether a minimum commitment with a penalty for breach is required depends on the size of the retailer's quasi-rents under the contract. The retailer's expected variable profit if it chooses

24

(P^*, x^*) is

$$
\begin{aligned}
E[\pi] &= (P^* - w_2)\overline{D} - \theta V(D) - (1-\theta)V(D^0) - r \\
&= (P^* - (P^* - a^*))\overline{D} - \theta V(D) - (1-\theta)V(D^0) - r \\
&= a^*\theta D + a^*(1-\theta)D^0 - \theta V(D) - (1-\theta)V(D^0) - r \\
&= a^* D^0 - V(D^0) + \theta \left(a^*[D - D^0] - [V(D) - V(D^0)] \right) - r \\
&= \int_0^{D^0} [a^* - v(q)]dq - r. \quad \text{(Using the definition of } a^*)
\end{aligned}
$$

(41)

The retailer can "defect" from choosing (P^*, x^*) by choosing a quantity of zero (e.g., by setting P very high and $x = 0$) and earning a profit of $-K$, or by choosing some price and investment that yield positive quantities in some states under the recognition that it will pay the higher price w_1 and potentially a penalty K when its sales are below $D^0(P^*, x^*)$. The expression for the retailer's defection profit is somewhat tedious to write. What is important is that w_1 and K can be set high enough that the retailer's best defection is to sell zero and earn $-K$. Thus, the contract T^* will support the first best outcome for sufficiently high w_1 if $E[\pi] \geq -K$. If the retailer's expected quasi-rents, $\int_0^{D^0} [a^* - v(q)]dq$, equal or exceed the retailer's investment cost $r(x^*)$, then the inequality is satisfied when $K = 0$, and no penalty (equivalently, no minimum commitment) is required. This is always true in Case 1, and it will be true in Case 2 if the retailer's expected quasi-rents exceed $r(x^*)$. If the retailer's expected quasi-rents are less than $r(x^*)$, then a minimum commitment and associated penalty is required to ensure that the retailer chooses (P^*, x^*). This establishes Parts 1 and 2 of the Proposition.

Part 3. I now establish the the general insufficiency of two-block tariffs. To simplify notation, assume $V = 0$, $r = 0$, and $D^0 = \alpha D$ (iso-elastic upstream investment). This case suffices to establish the insufficiency of two-block tariffs. Let w_1^T and w_2^T be the prices in the high-price and low-price blocks of a two-block tariff, and let q be the quantity that divides the blocks. In any first-best two-block tariff, $D^0 \leq q \leq D$; otherwise the tariff would be equivalent to a two-part tariff, which cannot yield the first best outcome. Given (w_1^T, w_2^T, q), the retailer solves

(42)
$$
\max_{(P,x)} \ P\overline{D}(P, x) - \theta[w_1^T q + w_2^T(D(P, x) - q)] - (1-\theta)w_1^T D^0(P, x).
$$

25

The first order condition with respect to P is

$$(43) \qquad \overline{D} + P\overline{D}_P - \theta w_2^T D_P - (1-\theta)w_1^T D_P^0 = 0.$$

The first-order condition for price at the first best outcome (from (31)) is

$$(44) \qquad \overline{D} + P\overline{D}_P - c\overline{D}_P = 0.$$

Two-block tariffs support the first best outcome only if (43) and (44) are both satisfied at (P^*, x^*). Subtracting (44) from (43) and evaluating at (P^*, x^*) gives

$$(45) \qquad \theta w_2^T D_P + (1-\theta)w_1^T D_P^0 = c\overline{D}_P.$$

Under iso-elastic upstream investment, (45) can be written

$$(46) \qquad \frac{\theta w_2^T + (1-\theta)\alpha w_1^T}{\theta + (1-\theta)\alpha} = c.$$

Using (46), we have

$$(47) \qquad w_1^T - c = \frac{\theta(w_1^T - w_2^T)}{\theta + (1-\theta)\alpha},$$

$$(48) \qquad w_2^T - c = -\frac{(1-\theta)\alpha(w_1^T - w_2^T)}{\theta + (1-\theta)\alpha}.$$

The highest investment an integrated firm would make under uncertain prospects is $(P^*-c)[D-D^0]$ The manufacturer will make the same investment only if

$$(49) \qquad (w_2^T - c)D + (w_1^T - w_2^T)q - (w_1^T - c)D^0 \geq (P^* - c)[D - D^0].$$

Straightforward algebra shows that condition (49) is also required for the manufacturer to make the highest investment an integrated firm would make under uncertain returns. Using (47), (48), and $D^0 = \alpha D$, condition (49) becomes

$$(50) \qquad (P^* - c)[D - D^0] \leq (w_1^T - w_2^T)\frac{[\theta + (1-\theta)\alpha]q - (1-\theta)\alpha D - \theta D^0}{\theta + (1-\theta)\alpha}$$

$$(51) \qquad = (w_1^T - w_2^T)\left[q - \frac{D^0}{\theta + (1-\theta)\alpha}\right]$$

$$(52) \qquad \leq (w_1^T - w_2^T)\left[D - \frac{D^0}{\theta + (1-\theta)\alpha}\right]$$

$$(53) \qquad = \frac{(w_1^T - w_2^T)\theta[D - D^0]}{\theta + (1-\theta)\alpha}.$$

26

Condition (52) follows from (51) because $q \leq D$. Since $(w_1^T - w_2^T)$ and $D - D^0$ are bounded,[23] the inequality (50) through (53) will be violated if θ is small, and the manufacturer will not make the first-best investment. **Q.E.D**

B. Intuition and Discussion

The basic intuition for all-units discounts under uncertain prospects and returns is similar to the intuition under deterministic returns. The all-units discount (plus the minimum commitment, if necessary) encourages the retailer to expand output, while keeping the wholesale price high enough to ensure manufacturer investment. In addition, the presence of risk provides a tool firms can exploit to achieve efficiency under a class of investment technologies (Cases 1 and 2) in which efficiency may not be possible when investment returns are deterministic. Under both uncertain prospects and returns, the retailer weighs the risk of failing to reach the quantity threshold against the potential gains from raising price and reducing its investment. If the penalty for failing to reach the threshold is high enough, then the retailer will price and invest to ensure that it reaches the discount threshold *even if successful investment by the manufacturer does not occur.* If price is the retailer's only decision, the penalty can be set high enough with an all-units discount in all cases. If the retailer also makes a demand-enhancing investment, a minimum commitment and penalty for breach may also be required if the investment cost is large relative to the retailer's quasi-rents.

Two-block tariffs are generally not sufficient to support the first best outcome. An optimal two-block tariff must set a measure of the *average* wholesale price equal to the manufacturer's marginal cost c to make the retailer the residual claimant to joint profits. If upstream investment costs are sufficiently high relative to the expected returns from upstream investment, then no such tariff exists that can also support upstream investment.

The role of the iso-elastic upstream investment assumption is not transparent from the proof of Proposition 5. Under the all-units discount contract T^*, the retailer can choose any ratio of P and x to achieve $D^0(P, x) = D^0(P^*, x^*)$. The first best outcome requires a particular ratio that weighs the marginal effects of P and x on both D^0 and D. The assumption that $D^0 = \alpha D$ is sufficient to

---

[23] I am assuming that $w_2^T \geq 0$. If this were not true, the retailer could increase its profit by ordering an unlimited amount of the input.

ensure that the retailer chooses the optimal ratio.

Several papers in the early agency literature identified conditions under which penalty schemes can be used to approximate or achieve first best outcome in various one-sided moral hazard problems.[24] The use of all-units discounts to encourage retailer output expansion here is analogous the role of penalties in those papers, although here the incentive contract must also deal with the manufacturer's moral hazard. The literature on partnerships[25] is in some ways a closer ancestor to the analysis here, as it examines conditions under which incentives can be aligned in partnerships between $N \geq 2$ players that face N-sided moral hazard. However, this literature did not explore the extent to which all-units discounts may arise as optimal contracts.

V. Upstream Entry

The policy debate surrounding all-units discounts centers on their potential role as a device to exclude competitors. To begin examining this issue, I introduce the potential for small scale entry into the upstream market, restricting attention to the case of deterministic investment returns. In stage one, the incumbent manufacturer and retailer agree to a contract, as before. In stage two, in addition to making investment and pricing decisions, the retailer considers whether to purchase q_E units from an alternative source of supply at a unit price of w_E. For simplicity, I assume that q_E and w_E are fixed. I will interpret the alternative source of supply as arising from an entrant willing to supply q_E at unit price w_E, although there are other valid interpretations.[26] If the contract induces the retailer to purchase q_E from the alternative source, I will say that the firms "accommodate upstream entry." Otherwise they "deter" upstream entry. For ease of notation, in this section I assume that the retailer incurs no production cost beyond what it pays the manufacturer, i.e., $V(Q) = 0 \ \forall Q$.

---

[24]See e.g. Mirrlees (1974, 1975, 1999), Gjesdal (1976), Holmstrom (1979, footnote 7), Lewis (1980), and Singh (1984).

[25]Examples include Williams & Radner (1988), Legros & Matsushima (1991), and Legros & Matthews (1993).

[26]For example, a competitive fringe may be able to supply q_E at price w_E, or the retailer may have the ability to integrate backward and produce under the same terms.

A. Accommodating Potential Upstream Entry

Suppose first that firms employ an effective all-units discount intended to accommodate upstream entry. The retailer must earn at least as much by accommodating entry and pricing and investing as expected under the all-units discount as it would earn by choosing not to accommodate entry and pricing and investing the same way. That is,

$$(54) \qquad (P - w_2)D(P, x) + (w_2 - w_E)q_E - r(x) \geq (P - w_2)D(P, x) - r(x).$$

This requires $w_E \leq w_2$. In addition, the retailer must earn at least as much by accommodating entry and pricing and investing as expected as it would earn by accommodating entry but optimizing against w_1. That is,[27]

$$(P - w_2)D(P, x) + (w_2 - w_E)q_E - r(x) \geq \max_{(P', x')} [(P' - w_1)D(P', x') - r(x')] + (w_1 - w_E)q_E$$

$$(55) \qquad \Longrightarrow (P - w_2)D(P, x) - r(x) - (w_1 - w_2)q_E \geq \hat{\pi}(w_1).$$

The manufacturer must also earn more by investing I^* than by choosing not to invest:[28]

$$(56) \qquad (w_2 - c)D(P, x) - m(I^*) + (w_1 - w_2)q_E \geq (w_1 - c)D^0(P, x).$$

Proposition 7 *Suppose investment is lumpy and investment returns are deterministic. Under either all-units discounts or two-block tariffs, the incumbent manufacturer and retailer will accommodate entry by a more efficient competitor.*

Proof: Since the analysis is similar to that for the case without entry, I will simply sketch the argument for all-units discounts. The argument for two-block tariffs parallels the argument in Proposition 4.

I first explain that (P^A, x^A) will be chosen if entry is accommodated. Fix $(P, x) = (P^A, x^A)$. Conditions (55) and (56) are the same as the participation constraints (7) and (8) in (AUDT) except for the terms involving $(w_1 - w_2)q_E$. Note that reducing w_2 raises the left hand side of (55)

---

[27]The retailer must also prefer accommodation over non-accommodation and optimizing against w_1, but it is easy to show that this will be true when (55) is satisfied and $w_E \leq w_2$.

[28]By an argument similar to that in Lemma 1, we can restrict attention to the case when $D(P, x) - q_E = q$. This implies that $D^0(P, x) - q_E < q$ which implies that if the manufacturer chooses not to invest, it will receive the price w_1 rather than w_2.

and lowers the left hand side of (56) by the same amount. Thus, for any value of w_1, there exists a value of w_2 such that (55) and (56) are satisfied at (P^A, x^A). In particular, they can be satisfied by setting $w_1 = w_1^A$ and setting $w_2 > c$ such that (55) and (56) hold. The incentive constraints on retail pricing and investment can be satisfied by choosing the appropriate shadow price ξ of output expansion, as in (AUDT). Thus, (P^A, x^A) is feasible under all-units discounts with entry. To do better, firms would have to adjust w_1. However, it is straightforward to verify from the first order conditions that w_1^A is still optimal. Thus, (P^A, x^A) are the optimal choices if entry is accommodated.

The joint profit of the incumbent manufacturer and retailer when entry is accommodated is $\Pi = (P^A - c)D(P^A, x^A) - (w_E - c)q_E - r(x^A) - m(I^*)$. If $w_E < c$, this will exceed the joint profits for the case without entry, so accommodating entry is optimal. The argument for why two-block tariffs are equivalent follows from arguments similar to those in Proposition 4. **Q.E.D.**

The rationale for accommodating entry by a more efficient competitor in this model is simple— it increases the joint profits of the incumbent and retailer. The substantive part of Proposition 7 is that efficient accommodation is supported by both all-units discounts and two-block tariffs.

B. Deterring Entry

Next I examine the optimal entry deterring contracts. Deterring small scale entry under either all-units discounts or two-block tariffs requires $w_2 = w_E$ (or w_2 just slightly less than w_E).

Consider first all-units discounts. The following conditions are necessary for entry deterrence:

(57)
$$(P - w_2)D(P, x) - r(x) \geq \max_{(P', x')} [(P' - w_1)D(P', x') - r(x')] + (w_1 - w_E)q_E = \hat{\pi}(w_1) + (w_1 - w_E)q_E,$$

(58)
$$(w_2 - c)D(P, x) - m(I^*) \geq (w_1 - c)D^0(P, x)$$

Condition (57) ensures that the retailer earns more by deterring entry and setting price and investment so as to achieve the all-units discount than it does by accommodating entry and optimizing against w_1. Condition (58) is identical to condition (8), which ensures that the manufacturer is willing to invest. [An argument analogous to that in Lemma 1 ensures that $\hat{U} = (w_1 - c)D^0$.]

30

Suppose $w_E < w_1^A$. (If $w_E > w_1^A$, then the optimal all-units discount for the case of no entry would automatically deter entry.) Then constraint (57) is tighter than the analogous constraint (7) that holds when entry is not possible, and constraint (58) is unchanged from (8). Thus, when there is potential entry at price $w_E < w_1^A$, all-units discounts that deter entry will distort pricing and investment decisions relative to the case of no entry whenever the constraints (57) and (58) are binding. If entry is deterred through all-units discounts, some investments that can be supported by all-units discounts and two-block tariffs absent the threat of entry will not be made when the threat of entry is present.

Next, consider the use of two-block tariffs to deter entry. Let (w_1^T, w_2^T) be the optimal two-block tariffs absent the threat of entry. There are two cases.

Case 1. Suppose first that $w_E \in [w_2^T, w_1^A]$. (Recall that $w_2^T < w_2^T + \xi^A = w_2^A < w_1^A$.) For all $w_E \in [w_2^T, w_1^A]$, the optimal two-block tariff absent the threat of entry will automatically deter entry and thus will remain optimal given the threat of entry. However, the optimal all-units discount absent the threat of entry does not deter entry. If firms decide to deter entry with an all-units discount and the incentive constraints bind, they will distort pricing and investment more than they would with two-block tariffs. If they decide to accommodate entry and the incentive constraints bind, some investments that could be supported absent the threat of entry will not be made. Either way, when $w_E \in [w_2^T, w_1^A]$, two-block tariffs are preferred (by the firms) to all-units discounts, and the preference is strict if the incentive constraints under entry-deterring all-units discount are binding.

Case 2. Next, suppose $w_E \in [c, w_2^T]$. In this case an entry deterring contract under both two-block tariffs and all-units discounts entails an additional distortion relative to the case of no entry. However, the optimal entry-deterring two-block tariff does better than the best entry-deterring all-units discount. I present the basic logic here and leave the formal details to the proof of Proposition 8 below.

Consider first the optimal entry-deterring two-block tariff. Given $w_2 = w_E$, the optimal tariff will set w_1 to minimize the sum of the defection profits. This is possible because q can be adjusted to distribute the defection profits so as to satisfy both defection constraints. On the other hand, consider an all-units discount with $w_2 = w_E$. In this case w_1 will not be chosen to minimize the sum of the defection profits. Under a binding all-units discount, it is not possible to adjust q independently of w_1 and w_2 to simply redistribute defection profits without distorting marginal incentives. Adjusting q affects decisions at the margin. Thus, when $w_E \in [c, w_2^T]$, deterring entry with two-block tariffs dominates (for the firms) deterring entry with all-units discounts.

The following proposition summarizes the discussion in this subsection.

Proposition 8 *Suppose investment is lumpy and investment returns are deterministic. Two-block tariffs are preferred (by the firms) over all-units discounts in deterring entry by small, less efficient competitors.*

Proof: See Appendix

VI.   Implications and Extensions

The antitrust policy debate over all-units discounts has been largely devoid of economic analysis explaining why firms use these tariffs. To the extent that theory guides policy, this guidance should be based on rigorous analysis that permits comparing equilibrium all-units discounts against a valid counterfactual using a well-specified economic model. I view this paper, along with that of Kolay et al. (2004), as taking initial steps in this direction.

While Kolay et al. examined the role of all-units discounts by a firm offering a menu of discounts to multiple buyers, this paper takes a step back to examine the simpler environment of bilateral monopoly, but with the additional complication of double moral hazard. I explored three cases in which all-units discounts arise in equilibrium: (1) lumpy upstream investment with determininstic returns; (2) uncertain upstream investment prospects that may become available to the upstream firm after contracts are signed; and (3) uncertain investment returns. Under bilateral monopoly, I showed that all-units discounts and continuous, two-block tariffs are optimal contracts in the first case, and I provided sufficient conditions for all-units discounts to support a first best outcome (and dominate two-block tariffs) in the second and third cases. In all cases, all-units discounts work by giving the retailer a strong incentive to expand output to reach the discount threshold, while keeping upstream margins high enough to encourage upstream investment.

Since all-units discounts arise in efficient vertical contracts between bilateral monopolists that face no threat of entry, it would be inappropriate to presume without evidence that the practice is anticompetitive simply because the firms employing such tariffs have market power. In fact, the benefits of all-units discounts may actually increase with the degree of market power, as this is precisely when sophisticated contracts have the largest effect on incentives.

The antitrust concern raised by all-units discounts is that they may raise barriers to entry and harm competition. To begin addressing this issue, I extended the model to allow for the possibility of small scale entry into the upstream market, focusing on the case of lumpy investment and deterministic returns. In this environment, I showed that the incumbent supplier and retailer will always accommodate entry by an equally- or more-efficient upstream competitor. Contrary to the conventional view, all-units discounts are not used in this model to deter such entrants. Further, I found that two-block tariffs are preferred by firms over all-units discounts as a device for deterring entry by less efficient competitors. Using all-units discounts to deter entry exacerbates distortions associated with double moral hazard. Two-block tariffs, by contrast, deter entry with smaller distortions than those created by all-units discounts.

The analysis of entry in this paper is admittedly limited to a special case—entry into a single market served by a downstream monopolist, at a small scale and exogenously-determined price, and with no potential for dynamic entry effects. Nonetheless, the analysis casts doubt on the argument that all-units discounts are a stronger entry deterrent than than other types of nonlinear contracts, at least when the contracting firms face double moral hazard. In the model here, all-units discounts may be used to accommodate entry by a more efficient competitor, but they are dominated by continuous tariffs in deterring entry by a less efficient competitor. While the gains from potentially anticompetitive entry deterrence might be greater in a richer environment, it is not clear why the relative desirability of all-units discounts and continuous tariffs as devices to deter entry would differ across environments.

One cannot conclude from the entry results that two-block tariffs raise anticompetitive concerns.

In the model here, deterring a less efficient entrant prevents the entrant from disrupting attempts to write sophisticated contracts that align pricing and investment incentives and solve or mitigate double moral hazard. This paper does not address welfare questions, in part because of the inherent ambiguities in determining whether contracts that align private incentives increase or decrease social welfare. It is easy to construct examples in which all-units discounts that dominate two-block tariffs expand investment, reduce double-marginalization, and increase social welfare. It is also possible to construct examples in which all-units discounts that expand investment decrease social welfare. Sorting through the conflicting effects is a tall order for antitrust authorities.

The model has some special features that deserve further investigation to understand their importance. The case of deterministic returns assumed two upstream investment choices. More generally, with $N > 2$ upstream investment choices, it seems clear that an N-point contract would be optimal, but it is not clear whether an N-price all-units discount or an N-block tariff can replicate the optimal contract. The uncertain prospects and returns cases also assumed two upstream investment choices. The results in these cases will hold under continuous investment if there is a positive probability that investment opportunities may not materialize in the uncertain prospects case, or may not be successful in the uncertain returns case. If the distribution of investment returns has no mass points, I conjecture that the results will hold if the distribution of returns is bimodal and increases (decreases) fast enough at the upper (lower) bounds of support, i.e., if the distribution in some sense looks enough like the case of lumpy investment.

REFERENCES

Bhattacharyya, Sugato, and Francine Lafontaine, "Double-Sided Moral Hazard and the Nature of Share Contracts," *The Rand Journal of Economics*, 26:4, Winter 1995, pp. 761-781.

Demski, Joel and David Sappington, "Resolving Double Moral Hazard Problems with Buyout Agreements," *The Rand Journal of Economics*, 22:2, Summer 1991, pp. 232-240.

European Commission, "Communication from the Commission – Guidance on the Commission's enforcement priorities in applying Article 82 of the EC Treaty to abusive exclusionary conduct by dominant undertakings," 2009.

Gjesdal, Froystein, "Accounting in Agencies," Stanford University, 1976, mimeo.

Greenlee, Patrick, and David Reitman, "Distinguishing Competitive and Exclusionary Uses of Loyalty Discounts," *The Antitrust Bulletin*, 50:3, Fall 2005, pp. 441-463.

Holmstrom, Bengt, "Moral Hazard and Observability," *The Bell Journal of Economics*, 10:1, Spring 1979, pp.74-91.

Holmstrom, Bengt, "Moral Hazard in Teams," *The Bell Journal of Economics*, 13:2, Autumn 1982, pp. 324-340.

Kolay, Sreya, Greg Shaffer, and Janusz A. Ordover, "All-Units Discounts in Retail Contracts," *Journal of Economics & Management Strategy*, 13:3, September 2004, pp.429-459.

Lewis, Tracy R., "Bonuses and Penalties in Incentive Contracting," *The Bell Journal of Economics*, 11:1, Spring 1980, pp. 292-301.

Legros, Patrick, and Hitoshi Matsushima, "Efficiency in Partnerships," *Journal of Economic Theory*, 55, 1991, pp. 296-322.

Legros, Patrick and Steven A. Matthews, "Efficient and Nearly-Efficient Partnership," *The Review of Economic Studies*, 60:3, July 1993, pp. 599-611.

Maskin, Eric and John Riley, "Monopoly with Incomplete Information," *Rand Journal of Economics*, 15:2, Summer 1984, pp. 171-196.

Mirrlees, J.A. "Notes on Welfare Economics, Information and Uncertainty," in M. Balch, D. McFadden and S. Wu (eds.) *Essays in Equilibrium Behavior under Uncertainty*, 1974, (Amsterdam: North Holland).

Mirrlees, J.A. "The Theory of Moral Hazard and Unobservable Behavior," Nuffield College, Oxford University, 1975, mimeo.

Mirrlees, J.A., "The Theory of Moral Hazard and Unobservable Behavior: Part I," *Review of Economic Studies*, 66, 1999, pp. 3-21.

Romano, Richard E., "Double Moral Hazard and Resale Price Maintenance," *Rand Journal of Economics*, 25:3, Autumn, 1994, pp. 455-466.

Singh, Nirvikar, "Moral Hazard with a Finite Number of States," *Economics Letters*, 16:1-2, pp.45-51.

Stoll, Lars A., "Price Discrimination and Competition," in *Handbook of Industrial Organization*, Vol 3, 2007, pp. 2221-2299.

Varian, Hal R., "Price Discrimination," in *Handbook of Industrial Organization*, Vol. 1, 1989, pp.597-654.

Wang, Susheng, "An Efficient Bonus Contract," mimeo, Department of Economics, Hong Kong University of Science and Technology, July 2009, Available at SSRN: http://ssrn.com/abstract=1479935.

Williams, Steven R. and Roy Radner, "Efficiency in Partnerships When the Joint Output is Uncertain," Discussion Paper No. 760, Northwestern University Department of Economics, February 1988.

Proof of Proposition 8: Case 1 requires no discussion beyond that in the text. The proof of Case 2 proceeds by showing that that the constraint set in the optimization problem with all-units discounts is a subset of the constraint set in the optimization problem with two-block tariffs. This implies that joint profits are at least as high under two-block tariffs as under all-units discounts.

The optimal entry-deterring all-units discount will have $w_2 = w_E$. The optimal contract solves

$$\text{(AUDT-E)} \quad \max_{(P,x,w_1,q,\xi)} (P-c)D(P,x) - V(D(P,x)) - r(x) - m(I^*) \quad s.t.$$

(59) $$(P-w_E)D(P,x) - V(D(P,x)) - r(x) \geq \hat{\pi}(w_1) + (w_1 - w_E)q_E,$$

(60) $$(w_E - c)D(P,x) - m(I^*) \geq (w_1 - c)D^0(P,x)$$

(61) $$D(P,x) + (P - v(D(P,x)) - w_E)D_P(P,x) + \xi D_P(P,x) = 0,$$

(62) $$(P - v(D(P,x)) - w_E)D_x(P,x) - r_x(x) + \xi D_x(P,x) = 0,$$

(63) $$D(P,x) \geq q,$$

(64) $$\xi(D(P,x) - q) = 0$$

Entry deterrence under two-block tariffs also requires $w_2 \leq w_E$. The optimal entry deterring contract under two-block tariffs solves

$$\text{(TBT-E)} \quad \max_{(P,x,w_1,q)} (P-c)D(P,x) - V(D(P,x)) - r(x) - m(I^*) \quad s.t.$$

(65) $$(P-w_E)D(P,x) - V(D(P,x)) - (w_1 - w_E)q - r(x) \geq \hat{\pi}(w_1) + (w_1 - w_E)q_E,$$

(66) $$(w_E - c)D(P,x) + (w_1 - w_E)q - m(I^*) \geq (w_1 - c)D^0(P,x),$$

(67) $$D(P,x) + (P - v(D(P,x)) - w_E)D_P(P,x) = 0,$$

(68) $$(P - v(D(P,x)) - w_E)D_x(P,x) - r_x(x) = 0,$$

(69) $$D(P,q) \geq q$$

(Note the implicit assumption in both problems that $\hat{U} = (w_1 - c)D^0$, as in the case with no entry. This is easy to establish.)

Let $(P^{AE}, x^{AE}, w_1^{AE}, \xi^{AE})$ solve (AUDT-E). I argue that the outcome (P^{AE}, x^{AE}) is feasible under two-block tariffs. To see this, let $w_2 = w_E - \xi^{AE}$ and $w_1 = w_1^{AE}$. Then constraints (67) through (69) are satisfied at (P^{AE}, x^{AE}). Constraints (65) and (66) can be written

(70) $$(P^{AE} - w_E)D^{AE} - V^{AE} - r^{AE}) + \left\{\xi^{AE}[D^{AE} - q] - (w_1^{AE} - w_E)q\right\} \geq \hat{\pi}^{AE},$$

37

(71) $(w_2^{AE} - c)D^{AE} - m(I^*) - \{\xi^{AE}[D^{AE} - q] - (w_1^{AE} - w_2^{AE})q\} \geq (w_1^{AE} - c)D^{0AE}$

where the superscript 'AE' indicates that all functions are evaluated at the equilibrium outcome under all-units discounts. Conditions (70) and (71) are identical to (59) and (60) if the term in curly braces is zero, which is feasible with

$$(72) \qquad q = \frac{\xi^{AE}}{w_1^{AE} - w_E + \xi^{AE}} D(P^{AE}, x^{AE}).$$

On the other hand, let $(P^{TE}, x^{TE}, w_1^{TE})$ solve (TBT-E). Differentiating the Lagrangian for (TBT-E), it is straightforward to show that w_1^{TE} is chosen such that $D(\hat{P}(w_1^{TE}), \hat{x}(w_1^{TE}) - q_E = D^0(P^{TE}, x^{TE})$, i.e., to minimize the sum of the defection profits. However, differentiating the Lagrangian in (AUDT-E) indicates that the optimal choice of w_1 under all-units discounts is generally different than w_1^{TE} and does not minimize the sum of the defection profits. (Unlike the case with no entry, the Lagrangian multipliers on the defection constraints are generally different. They must be equal for the w_1 to minimize the sum of the defection profits.) It follows that joint profits are higher under two-block tariffs, and that some investments that can be supported with two-block tariffs cannot be supported with all-units discounts. **Q.E.D.**

www.ingramcontent.com/pod-product-compliance
Lightning Source LLC
Chambersburg PA
CBHW081241170526
45165CB00009B/3141